2 ★

LOS ANGELES

hollywood

 3

LOS ANGELES

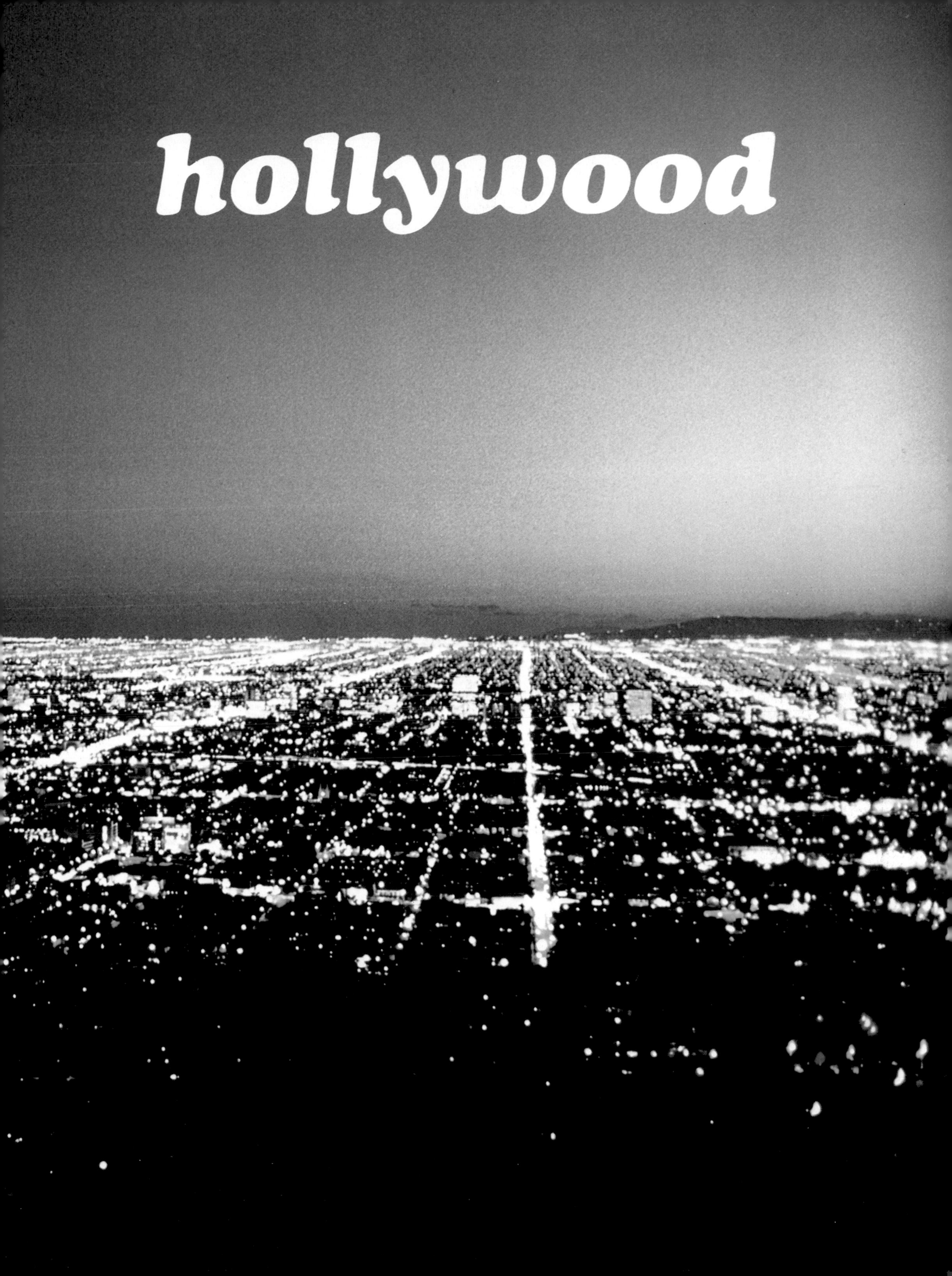
hollywood

Published by

Randy Collings Productions

Box 8658 • Holiday Station
Anaheim, California 92802

Featuring the
Photography of
Craig Aurness
with
James Blank, Roy Murphy
and Don Tormey

Written by
Randy Collings

LOS ANGELES
hollywood

Golden State Library
Volume Two

Editor .... Randy Collings
Design and Graphics .... Randy Collings
Illustrations .... N. Kay Stevenson

Special thanks to the Academy of Motion Picture Arts and Sciences, the American Broadcasting Company, Inc., Autoexpo '79, the California Historical Society, Cal Trans, Casablance Record and Filmworks, the CBS Television Network, the Church of Jesus Christ of Latter-day Saints, the Forum, the Los Angeles County Museum of Natural History, the Los Angeles Dodgers, Magic Mountain, Metro-Goldwyn-Mayer Inc., the Metropolitan Water District of Southern California, the National Broadcasting Company, Inc., the Pasadena Tournament of Roses Association, Plough Inc., the Santa Catalina Island Company, Twentieth Century Fox Film Corporation, Universal Picture Studios, Warner Bros. Inc., Westlake Village, and the countless other companies and individuals who have helped to make this publication possible.

Cover photo—LA at dusk by Craig Aurness. Title page—Mann's Chinese Theater by James Blank. Opening spreads in order: LA by night—Craig Aurness, Sunset along the Pacific Coast—Roy Murphy, Pomona Valley and San Gabriel Mountains—Roy Murphy, LA skyline at sunset—Craig Aurness. Photographs this page courtesy of the Academy of Motion Picture Arts and Sciences.

Randy Collings Productions

© ACADEMY OF MOTION PICTURE ARTS AND SCIENCES

LOS ANGELES
hollywood

Contents

Randy Collings Productions

© CBS-artwork by Ren Wicks

Introduction

This is the story of a city unequaled by any other major metropolis in today's world—a truly remarkable community already struggling with the challenges of the 21st century.

Herein lies a grand success story in which one encounters the character of a beautiful and dynamic personality who rises to meet every challenge, climbing one mountain after another, achieving fame and fortune far beyond her wildest expectations—and yet not without having made the sacrifice, paid the dues, and gone the distance.

A far cry from the ramshackled pueblo of yesteryear, she stands before the world today as a prototype of things to come.

In this marvelous volume of showcase art, photography, and text, we have endeavored to do justice to a woman who is at times so camp and yet so noble—Los Angeles.

—Randy Collings

1. In the beginning...

Painting by George Knight. Courtesy of the Los Angeles
County Museum of Natural History.

American Lion *and sabre-toothed cat. Artwork courtesy of the George C. Page Museum.*

While extensive glaciers were carving out the magnificent Yosemite Valley to the north, mammoths and mastodons were converging upon Southern California by the thousands, as if fleeing to a sort of prehistoric vacation paradise in the tropics, waiting out the freezing temperatures and winter storms of a prolonged Ice Age.

Today, in a city where ever since the advent of the motion picture industry nothing seems unusual or out of the ordinary, it is debatable whether a giant elephant, 13 feet high at the shoulder, standing at the corner of Hollywood and Vine, would attract more than a casual glimpse from a local studio executive buzzing by in his 450 SL. Scientists theorize that the massive migrations of prehistoric wildlife to this temperate coastal plain began about 38,000 years ago, when the land first rose above sea level. Man apparently appeared upon the scene about the same time, as attested to by

Imperial Mammoth *and Mastodon. Artwork courtesy of the George C. Page Museum.*

the carbon dating guestimation of fossils and a local legend which speaks of the Indians colonizing in the new lands as they rose from the sea.

During these first days of Los Angeles, the climate was somewhat more humid, creating a landscape similar to that found in Northern California today. Forests of pine and juniper flourished amid vast, rolling plains and grassy prairies. Springs and swamps collected and distributed moisture to sustain the luxuriant growth of the valley floor. Beneath the waters of one such source, however, asphalt from an underground oil deposit bubbled up through the marshy terrain, emitting the unpleasant odor of tar. As beasts of the valley would venture into this black cauldron, they oftentimes became entrapped in the sticky substance. Unable to free themselves, they fell prey to predators like the saber-toothed cat and the American lion, who not infrequently would sink, with their prey, into the murky depths of the tar pits.

Acting as an historical catch-all these tar pits in modern times have provided 20th-century scientists with the most extensive collection of Ice Age fossils in the world.

About 8,000 years ago the earth's climate began to change drastically. The Ice Age came to an end as warm ocean currents brought balmy subtropical weather to the extreme northern and southern hemispheres. In Southern California the climate grew arid. Heavy rains diminished, inland seas dried up, and the woodlands receded. As the grasslands disappeared, the larger herbivores, too, began to vanish, aided in their inevitable extinction by hunting parties of Shoshone Indians. By the time Europeans arrived upon the scene, all that remained were the elk, antelope, deer and grizzly.

A prehistoric *hunting party (left) attacks an Imperial mammoth as it struggles to escape from the La Brea Tar Pits. Painting courtesy of the George C. Page Museum.*

By 1770 the human population of Los Angeles numbered not more than 6,000. To save these souls from their primitive, ignorant sins and to lay claim to and colonize the land for a faraway, civilized nation became the motive that brought LA out of its prehistoric isolation and into the age of discovery and enlightenment. Since as early as the 16th century, sailing vessels from Europe had occasionally appeared in the coastal waters of California. Their occupants, usually from the colonies of Spain, came ashore only for the briefest of stays; and although they found the region to be agreeable and pleasant, they made no efforts to colonize, cultivate, or otherwise improve.

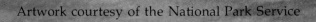

Not until the challenge arose to compete for the rich lands of the West Coast were serious efforts made on the part of Spain to build pueblos, erect presidios, and convert the neophytes. In an effort to keep Russians, Britons, and Portugese from laying claim to this vast frontier, the King of Spain sent an extensive expedition into Alta California to secure his right to the land.

In August of 1769 this first party of Europeans, under the command of one Gaspar de Portola, arrived at the perimeters of the Los Angeles basin and described it as a spacious plain which rolled westward into the distance. They marveled that they could not see its end. An interesting note is that when the party reached the present-day LA suburb of El Monte, they were frightened by a tremendous earthquake, an occurrence which has since become as synonomous with the name of the city as Hollywood itself.

In August of 1771 members of the earlier expedition returned to the Los Angeles area, along with several fathers from the Franciscan order of the Catholic Church. They came to establish the fourth religious outpost in a chain of missions that would soon stretch along the entire length of the present-day state of California.

The founding of the San Gabriel Mission was followed in 1781 with the establishment of a small pueblo, one and one-half leagues distant from the Franciscans' settlement. Eleven families, recruited from the Spanish colonies in northern Mexico, gathered near the site of present-day Olvera Street on November 19 of that fateful year and christened their settlement "El Pueblo de Nuestra Senora la Reina de Los Angeles de Porciuncula," which simply means "The Town of the Queen of the Angels."

Another mission was founded little more than a decade later in nearby San Fernando.

Artwork courtesy of the California Historical Society

Roping a grizzly *by James Walker.*
Artwork courtesy of the California Historical Society.

Following Mexico's liberation from Spanish rule in 1821, large tracts of mission lands were awarded to a number of distinguished war heroes. Ranchos were established, and soon a prosperous hide and tallow industry developed. Vast herds of cattle roamed the rangelands that had once been inhabited by bison and mastodons. Colorful rodeos were held each year to separate cattle belonging to the missions from those of the Spanish land barons. During this time of festivity, the locals indulged in a gruesome sport—that of pitting a wild bull against a chained grizzly. Our present-day "bear and bull market" stock exchange expressions were thus originated. Inhabiting the region in great numbers, the mighty bear was driven to extinction through such sport and unchecked hunting.

For several brief decades a period of wealth, security, and optimism prevailed among the newly established aristrocracy of rancheros and caballeros. Isolated from the rest of the civilized world, they lived a low-key existence in an idyllic pastoral setting. This picturesque Rancho Era has since become so deeply etched into the heritage of the Golden State that to this day it reappears in local names as well as in the design of suburban homes, churches, and even shopping centers.

Yankee sailors and fur trappers from the new American nation on the opposite side of the continent began arriving in increasingly large numbers. By 1846 the conflict between cultures had erupted into a war; and on January 13, 1847, the governor of Alta California surrendered his province to the United States.

During this time of transition, great injustices were inflicted upon the members of the proud Californio aristocracy as they stood by, helpless to defend their estates against the American court system. Land was what the

Yankees wanted — and would have. Land was the cornerstone upon which the Californio society was built. The "gringos," who measured real estate by the acre, could never fully understand a society in which land had been measured by the square league.

In Los Angeles, business boomed briefly as Yankee entrepreneurs flowed into the newly acquisitioned territory and began to establish enterprises of their own. Lawlessness prevailed, however, as angry Mexican bandidos harassed and pillaged the flocks, herds, and shops of the hated Americans. For many years, contentions and prejudices plagued the pueblo as it struggled to become a thriving metropolis. Eventually, the Spanish and American cultures married in Los Angeles and gave birth to a society well endowed with the best of each parent.

Los Angeles—Queen of the cow country, *as portrayed by James Walker.*
Artwork courtesy of the California Historical Society.

Agrarian Los Angeles *(above and opposite page) during the height of her citrus raising era. Artwork courtesy of the California Historical Society.*

The citrus industry began to develop as early as 1870 when navel oranges were introduced into the area from Brazil. Padres at the San Gabriel Mission had long since proved the feasibility of the industry after having planted LA's first orchard in 1804.

These first crops did amazingly well in the mild Mediterranean climate of the Southland and attracted the interests of many a gentleman farmer. By the turn of the century, "Orange Gold" had lured more settlers to California than the original Gold Rush of '49.

In 1880 a land boom began, the likes of which had never before been seen in all of California. Of the more than 100 towns plotted and sold in the real estate frenzy, more than 60 vanished into oblivion as the entire speculatory scheme collapsed in a confusing return of paper profits.

In spite of the overselling of real estate, the city continued to grow and prosper. In 1899 the construction of a long breakwater off the coast of LA converted the mudflats of San Pedro into a world port.

Turn of the century LA, *with all of the excitement of a booming petroleum industry (above) and the festivities surrounding the opening of the floodgates on the California aqueduct (opposite page). Photographs courtesy of the California Historical Society.*

Oil was also discovered during this time. Within six years over 3,000 wells had been established in West Los Angeles alone.

In 50 short years the population had grown from a mere 1,600 individuals to well over 100,000. With vast citrus orchards laid out across the basin and heavy industrialization beginning as a result of the newly formed petroleum industry, Angelenos became acutely aware that their water sources were insufficient to supply a rapidly growing metropolitan area.

In 1913 the floodgates were opened on a $25 million dollar aqueduct. Gallons of precious water flowed into the arid Los Angeles basin, having traveled a journey of over 240 miles from the snowfields of the High Sierra. In years to come, more such supply lines would be established, all of which eventually converted the dusty plain into a tropical arboretum even more verdant than its original prehistoric landscape.

This is the great picture upon which the famous comedian has worked a whole year.
6 reels of Joy.
Charles Chaplin
IN
"THE KID"
Written and directed by Charles Chaplin
A First National Attraction

During the early years of the 20th century, in distant New York, a fascinating art form that would come to be known as the motion picture was beginning to develop into a major industry. Owners of patents on motion picture equipment formed a protective trust to safeguard their inventions. This overzealous control of the industry seriously handicapped filmmakers, hindering the genius and creative potential of those early artists. Lured by the perpetual sunshine, dramatic settings, and varied geography of Southern California, filmmakers began to take refuge in Los Angeles—far from the all powerful control of "The Trust." Here the art form of film began to take hold and flourish as one of the world's most affluent business ventures.

Not until the success of Mary Pickford, America's Sweetheart, did the idea of promoting a celebrity as well as the film itself occur to the producers of motion pictures. The "Star" system evolved, and studios began choosing stories that would enhance the public image of their particular actor or actress.

As motion picture studios began to appear up and down Sunset and Santa Monica Boulevards, another industry was beginning to "flex its wings" nearby. In a small office behind a barber shop on Santa Monica Boulevard, plans were being made to create a fleet of planes that could airlift equipment and circle the globe. By the early 1930's the aerospace industry had already become a major element in the LA industrial scene.

John W. Considine, Jr. presents

RUDOLPH VALENTINO in "The Son of the Sheik"

a Sequel to The Sheik'

with VILMA BANKY

from the novel by E. M. HULL as Adapted to the Screen by FRANCES MARION

A GEORGE FITZMAURICE PRODUCTION · UNITED ARTISTS PICTURE ·

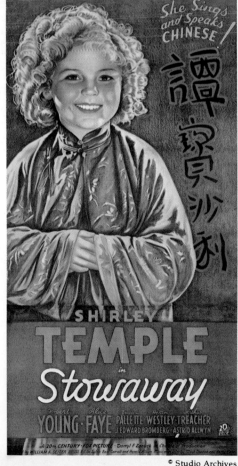

She Sings and Speaks CHINESE!

譚寶沙刺

SHIRLEY TEMPLE in Stowaway

YOUNG · FAYE PALLETTE WESTLEY TREACHER J. Edward Bromberg · Astrid Allwyn

A 20th CENTURY-FOX PICTURE · Darryl F. Zanuck

a DAVID O. SELZNICK production

Starring

CLARK GABLE and VIVIEN LEIGH

World War II brought thousands in uniform to the West Coast. Finding the climate agreeable and the opportunities of the post-war industrial boom lucrative, many decided to stay.

By 1950 the population of Los Angeles numbered in the millions. Agriculture and petroleum were waning as major industries while Hollywood, aerospace, and a myriad of manufacturing enterprises continued to bring more and more affluence to the community. Revolutionary changes in the Los Angeles landscape became increasingly apparent. Lost in surge after surge of immigrations, much of the heritage of Spanish California became obliterated. Virtually overnight, a modernistic city unlike any other in the world grew out of the Los Angeles plain.

Photograph courtesy of the California Historical Society

Intricate networks of freeways connected a sprawling metropolis that seemed to know no end. Although always plagued with a natural climatic condition that prevented the normal circulation of air currents, contaminents from the urban explosion below made the atmosphere almost unbreathable. A new word for the LA mixture of smoke and fog was formed, and "smog" became the city's greatest dilemma.

An iconoclastic generation, naive but outspoken, tagged LA as a city of "flash, cash, and trash," synthetic in every sense of the word. From a cultural viewpoint, they chided, she was the home of absolutely nothing. Undaunted by her detractors, the Queen of the Angels emerged from the turbulent 60's having consolidated her position as national trendsetter. Outdistancing her critics in their own causes, she became a leader in urban development and environmental research, as well as a cultural center hailed the world over by artists of every discipline.

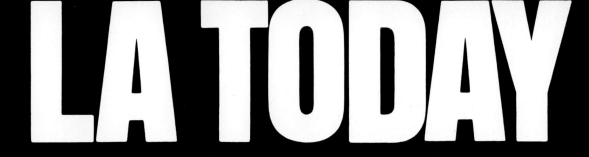

LA TODAY

Today, Los Angeles stands as a city unequaled in scope and splendor. When compared with the Big Apple, the Big Orange always seems to hold her own. Unquestionably one of the most exciting communities in today's world, it would be virtually impossible to present her countless virtues and vices in a volume of this size. Nonetheless, a brief physical description is in order.

Approaching the LA basin by air on a clear day creates one of the most stirring sights that one may ever see, particularly on an evening flight when the valley is ablaze with a dazzling sea of lights. Although frequently obliterated by thick marine air and smog, the panorama of a super-city surrounded by rugged mountains, rolling hills, and offshore islands is unquestionably one of the most spectacular vistas in the world. A semi-tropical metropolis of palm trees, sky scrapers, oil derricks, motion picture studios, and aerospace compounds, Los Angeles sprawls out across an area of nearly 40,000 square miles, housing 11 million people in over 140 different communities.

The only marketplace of its kind, she boasts of over 20,000 industrial establishments and trades with no less than 163 nations, serving as headquarters for countless international business operations.

LA's lifeline is its network of aqueducts that bring millions of gallons of water daily to supply the needs of the second largest community in America. Dangerously fragile and yet surprisingly efficient, these long, slender canals reach out across the deserts to tap faraway sources along the Colorado River and in the Sierra Nevada Mountains of Central and Northern California. Further solutions to the problems of supplying a city of this size with adequate water and power are currently under study.

The Colorado River Aqueduct *stretches across the desert carrying millions of gallons of precious water to supply the needs of a growing super city. Photograph courtesy of the Metropolitan Water District of Southern California.*

In 75 years the growth of Los Angeles has surpassed that of any other area in man's history. The world's most outstanding example of a purely 20th century community, its city-scape as we see it today has emerged almost entirely during the post-World War II era. Such phenominal growth continues as LA assumes its role as the production center and primary marketplace of the Pacific Rim.

PHOTOGRAPH BY CRAIG AURNESS

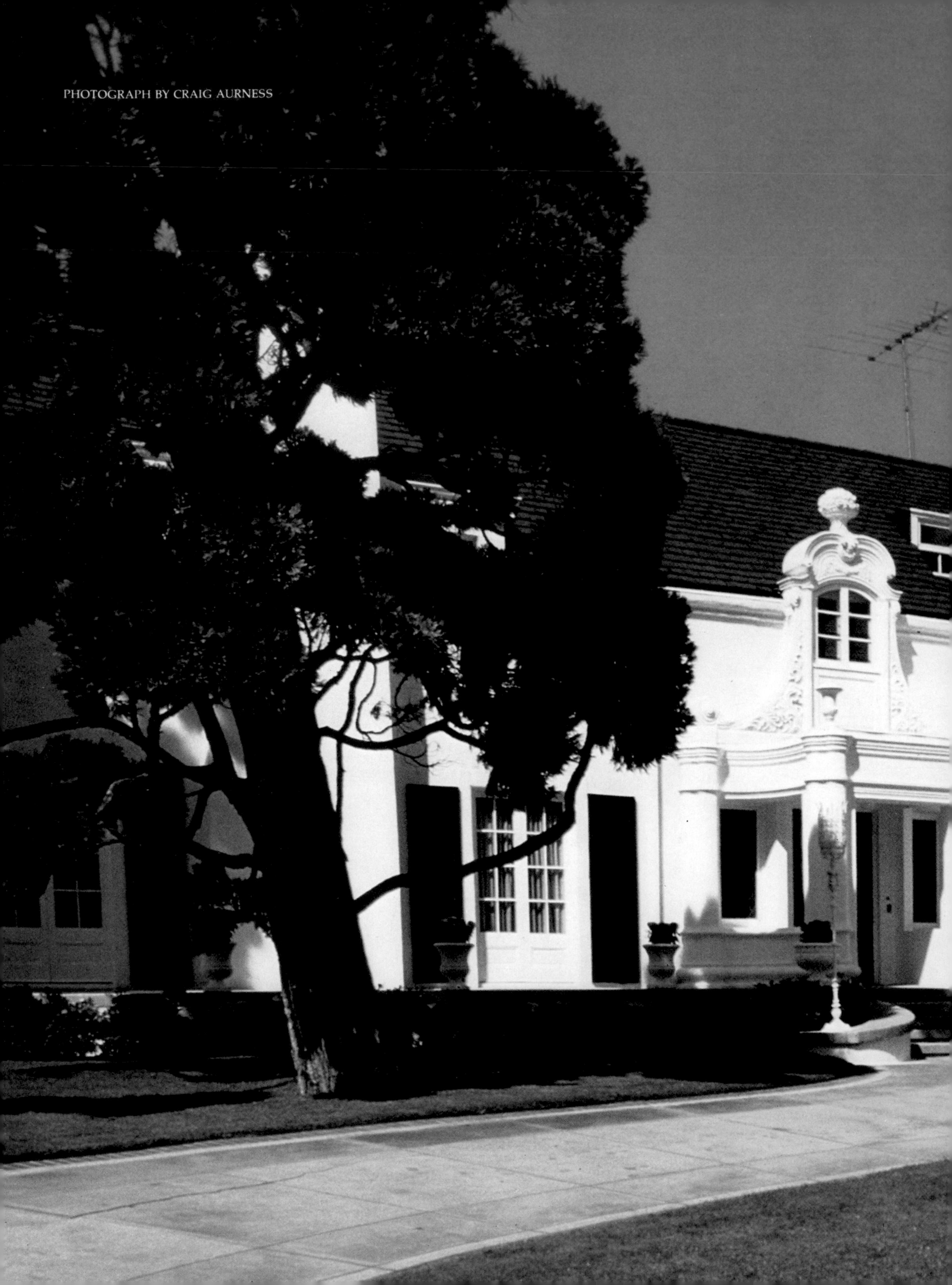

When attempting to comprehend the vastness of the City of the Angels, it is important to remember that she is the first American city to have come of age following the advent of the automobile. Where other communities have adapted themselves to the car, in LA the reverse has been the case— the car determined the development of the city and its suburbs.

Perhaps the single most important possession of the typical Angeleno family is its means of transportation. Los Angeles alone boasts of possessing

more automobiles than any other nation in the world, excepting the United States itself. With its advanced freeway system, distances have come to be measured in minutes rather than miles. Here, in the Commuter Capital of the World, Angelenos will frequently spend three hours a day driving to and from work and will think nothing of driving 60 miles round trip to see a movie. Elevated to the status of a hedonistic diety, the auto provides city dwellers and urbanites with the ultimate escape mechanism—a toy that can propel its driver at will into the hinterlands of the vast California landscape, far from the pressures of home. With such an ideology at work, it is not surprising to learn that famous foreign car manufacturers have zeroed in on this lucrative market, selling more of their wares here than at home.

A visitor to Los Angeles has the immediate impression that he is in the Rolls Royce capital of the world, with Porsche and Mercedes Benz running neck and neck for second place. This is not to say that nobody in LA drives a Pinto, quite the contrary. But Angelenos have a way of expressing their personalities through their automobiles, and the guest is often fascinated by the endless parade of customized adaptations to the otherwise average everyday run-of-the-mill car.

Indeed, not the geography but the personality of this community's population sets LA apart as one of the world's greatest, if not at times the most bizarre, cities. An international mosaic in the true sense of the word, one would have a difficult task to find a nationality or religion that is not represented here. In addition to the light skinned, but frequently suntanned, Anglo Saxons, Los Angeles is also home of the second largest Mexican and Jewish communities in the world. The largest Japanese colony outside of Japan resides here, as well as the largest and most dynamic black community in America.

LA is a magnet for scientists and technologists, containing a significant colony of world-renowned researchers and Nobel Prize winners.

BILL MINTOR

From a futuristic control center *fed by a complex network of computers Caltrans employees together with the California Highway Patrol supervise the flow of traffic on the world's busiest freeway system.*

CRAIG AURNESS

Mayor Tom Bradley, *first of a black minority to be elected by a non-black majority to serve a major American city.*

Fantasy has always flourished here and continues to do so as the dream machine of Hollywood has scattered itself out across the suburbs from Burbank to Anaheim, casting a hue of magic upon an otherwise ordinary environment.

Residents of one of the most affluent communities in America, most Angelenos are employed in aerospace, manufacturing, public service, or entertainment. Despite all the myths of a laid back lifestyle, most live life at a hectic pace here. This is a city that means business. Nevertheless, its

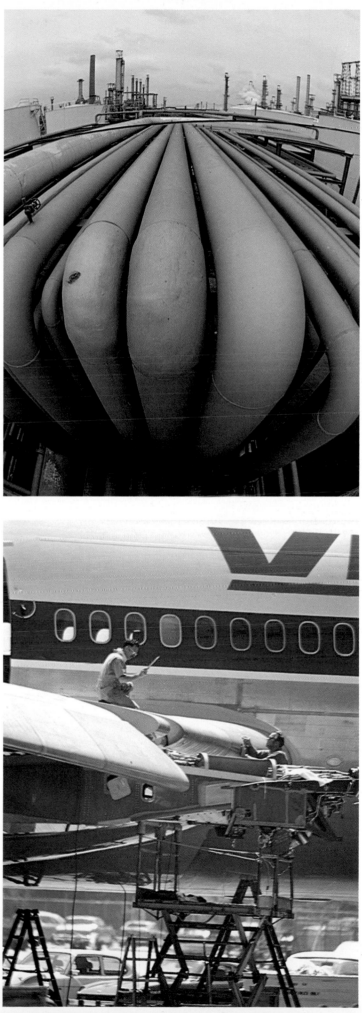

WILSON NORTH

DON TORMEY

euphoric environment of perennial sunshine and balmy sea breezes quickly eases pressures, and one in no way encounters the uptight atmosphere that seems to pervade most other communities of comparable size. Indeed, one of the greatest amenities of LA is that it is so easy to get away from. Magnificent high- country retreats in the Sierra, posh desert resorts like

Palm Springs, and scenic coastal communities such as Santa Barbara — all are within a few hours drive from the heart of the city. For all of this — and much more — many have come to LA and decided to stay.

A community of aspiring young businessmen, chic sunlovers, retired movie stars, innovative industrialists, millionaires — above all a community full of opportunity, challenges, and potential — Los Angeles today is what much of the world hopes to be tomorrow.

PHOTOGRAPH BY CRAIG AURNESS

2. The Coast

CRAIG AURNESS

CRAIG AURNESS

RANDY COLLINGS

Immortalized for time and all eternity by the surfing sounds of the Beach Boy era, LA's 74 miles of sea coast encompass some of the most exciting scenic and recreational attractions on the western seaboard. From a rugged shoreline north of Malibu to an endless expanse of white sand at Long Beach, this Pacific playground attracts literally millions of surfers, sunworshippers, seafaring men, and aquatic sports enthusiasts each year.

Southern Californians' love for the sun and the sea never ceases. With its windswept swells and pounding surf, the free spirit of the Pacific seems symbolic of the adventurous nature inherent in each one of us. During the chilly months of winter, when the ocean breeze is brisk and water temperatures are on the cool side, bathers don wet suits and brave the icy

CRAIG AURNESS

CRAIG AURNESS

CRAIG AURNESS

chill for sessions of swimming and surfing. As the warmer summer season approaches, a mass migration to the coast begins as thousands decorate the sand with a brightly colored checkerboard of beach towels and bathing suits.

There is something awesome and aesthetically dramatic about a giant megalopolis that stops abruptly at the very edge of an endless sea of blue—an unpeopled ocean stretching out in all its vastness to the western horizon beyond. Here, the continent ends; and for many this has become the end of their search for a place in the sun, the end of their own personal rainbow. And from the looks of the suntans and smiles on the beach, it appears as if they have, in actuality, discovered that fabled pot of gold—that California dream.

Surfing *at Malibu.*

Just south of Point Mugu, along the Ventura County line, the Pacific Coast Highway officially enters Los Angeles, winding its way beneath steep bluffs and rocky outcroppings of ancient sandstone. Here, the southern slope of the Santa Monica Mountains plummets into the sea, rising again just off shore to form the island of Santa Catalina. Spread out intermittantly between the coves and rocky clefts of this dramatic coastline are beautiful white sand beaches— among them Zuma, the largest in the County, and Point Dume, with its throngs of surfers and fascinating tide pools.

At Malibu, LA's most famous beach town, mountains and shoreline merge to create an environment coveted the world over. Along the beach at what is referred to locally as "the colony," beautiful homes rise in a row, one after another, each with its own private access to the Pacific. Above the coast, on the summits of the surrounding hillsides, stand many more spectacular homes, all with their own breathtaking vistas of land and sea. Many of these picturesque dwellings belong to motion picture, television, and sports celebrities. Each affords an insight into the personality of its owner, as no two are alike.

Stretching out across acres of Malibu hill country is the beautiful campus of Pepperdine University. Only one of more than 80 different schools of higher education in Los Angeles, Pepperdine is by far the County's most scenic. So outstanding is its setting, with student dormitories resembling Mediterranean condominiums and red-tile roofed lecture halls, that since the school's opening in 1972, it has served as the site for countless television network and motion picture productions.

Beyond Malibu, on a bluff overlooking the sea, stands the magnificent estate of the Late J. Paul Getty, one-time billionaire and oil magnate. Designed to mirror an ancient Roman villa, the beautiful grounds and buildings were bequeathed to the citizens of Los Angeles prior to Mr. Getty's death and today serve as home for several magnificent collections of art and sculpture. The estate is open five days a week for public inspection. There is no charge for parking or admission, another demonstration of Mr. Getty's generosity. For a nominal fee, one can hire the services of a 90-minute audio cassette tour, narrated by the Museum director, which highlights major objects in each collection and presents a history of the estate itself.

Only a short distance away stands the home of another well-known American figure, Will Rogers—humorist, lecturer, patriot. Today, his estate is maintained as part of the California State Park System. Nearby stretches a mile-long beach that also bears his name.

Exploring a cave (top photo) north of Malibu. *Pepperdine university (middle photo). An early morning session on the beach with a local surfing instructor (bottom photo). Photographs by Craig Aurness*

The J. Paul Getty Museum *(both photos this page) near Malibu, houses many magnificent works of art and affords a commanding view of the Pacific below.*

Santa Monica's Pacific playground (*top photo*) *on a typical summer day. Fishing pier (lower left corner photo) at Malibu, and local "California" girl (below).*

CRAIG AURNESS

Beautiful Pacific Palisades (top photo) one of LA's most attractive seaside communities. Summer heat and cool water temperatures lure residents to the shore (lower right corner photo). "The Beach" has always been a favorite meeting place among Southern California youth (below).

CRAIG AURNESS

CRAIG AURNESS

Santa Monica typifies the bucolic California of fame and legend. Its miles of white sand beaches, carnival-type playground along the pier, and lush green suburbs—all bathed in year-round sunshine—have appeared time after time as the setting for many a media production.

Also famous for the Mr. America contest, Santa Monica is home of Muscle Beach and Gold's Gym, where the sport of bodybuilding is taken seriously—producing modern-day gladiators the likes of Arnold Scharwzanneger and Lou Ferrigno.

In 1905 Abbot Kinney, a wealthy Easterner, decided to re-create the romantic charm of Venice, Italy, in Southern California. Canals were dug, bridges constructed, and gondolas imported, all following the schematic appearance of the development's Mediterranean counterpart. Venice today is not much more than a quiet suburb nestled along the southern California coast. Artists have gathered here, creating a colony of significant size. Their presence is everywhere evident as magnificent outdoor murals and private galleries add color and charm to an otherwise typical neighborhood.

Just beyond Venice lies Marina del Rey, the largest and busiest small craft harbor in the world. Dockside amenities include several of LA's finest restaurants.

Nearby begins the scenic 14-mile stretch of Palos Verdes, an uplift in the shoreline formed by ancient earthquake activity. Most popular of all attractions on the peninsula is the aquatic playground of Marineland. Here, guests can experience close contact with denizens of the deep and enjoy outstanding shows and attractions, each featuring a star from Davy Jones' locker.

On a clear day, the Palos Verdes panorama affords a spectacular view of Santa Catalina Island, a series of mountain peaks that rise above the calm Pacific, creating an isolated retreat for both man and beast. In addition to a significant colony of sea lions, the island is also home to over 400 buffalo. Clear waters and rich kelp beds make this an ideal location for deep-sea fishing, with shoreline grottos creating a virtual paradise for scuba and skin divers. Most of the activity on Catalina is centered around Avalon Bay. At one time a popular vacation destination and hideaway for men like Zane Grey and William Wrigley, the town today continues to play host to thousands of guests annually. The magnificent casino on the waterfront and many other picturesque settings make this area a favorite summer retreat for many Angelenos.

Ports O'Call (top photos) attracts locals and out of towners alike to its charming New England style shops and restaurants. Tuna boats (left) at San Pedro await their next voyage while cargo ships nearby (below) divulge their treasures gathered from around the world and prepare to take on export items manufactured in Los Angeles and the West Coast.

JAMES BLANK

The Vincent Thomas Bridge (above) spans San Pedro Harbor. Drilling for petroleum (right) is still a major industry in Long Beach (below), LA's fifth largest community.

DON TORMEY

CRAIG AURNESS

PHOTOS: DON TORMEY

Spanning LA's international sea port at San Pedro is the beautiful Vincent Thomas Memorial Bridge. A drive across it provides the motorist with a grand view of one of the world's busiest harbors. At Ports O'Call the charm and flavor of a New England fishing village has been successfully transplanted to the subtropical Los Angeles scene. A myriad of specialty shops and fine restaurants make this a favorite destination among locals and out-of-towners alike.

The magnificent British luxury liner, Queen Mary, sits stately at her permanent berth across the harbor in Long Beach. A vital petroleum-producing community since the turn of the century, Long Beach is the fifth largest community in Los Angeles, playing host to millions of guests each year with its huge arena and convention center, seaside carnival, mighty steamship, and annual Long Beach Grand Prix. This latter event, only several years old, has already been acclaimed as one of the world's most spectacular auto racing exhibitions.

The Coast, with all its variety and scenic splendor, provides Los Angeles with a natural boundary to its urban expansion. Sitting as it does on the edge of the world's last great frontier, LA enjoys an uncluttered horizon and cool sea breezes that create a euphoric environment wherein talent is born and ingenuity nourished. Much remains to be learned from the Sea. Abundant resources and rich natural treasures will undoubtedly prove a boon to the city's economy in the years ahead. For all its economic advantages, however, perhaps the most priceless gift of the Pacific is found in the inspiration and emotional release that it provides for the individual. Many have come to the Sea for answers. All have left refreshed.

CRAIG AURNESS

3. Mountain

Wilderness

PHOTOGRAPHED EXCLUSIVELY BY ROY MURPHY

Rising from near sea level to a height of over 10,000 feet, the San Gabriel Mountains stand like timbered walls— a formidable stone barrier— shielding the temperate coastal region below from the sweltering heat of the Mojave Desert beyond. Between the ancient walls of these awesome mountains, one encounters an alpine environment of stately pine and fir, wooded canyons, rushing creeks, cascading waterfalls, and delicate wildflowers.

Originally christened "Sierra Madre" (Mother of Mountains) by the Spanish padres, these ancient mountains later assumed the name of the mission that was established at their base. For many years they were considered an impenetrable fortress transversed only by two obscure Indian paths and inhabited by behemoth grizzly bears. They remained still and

unviolated, trespassed only occasionally by bandidos and horse- rustlers seeking sanctuary in the remote meadows of their high country.

Gold mining in Southern California began as early as 1842, bringing miners to the threshold of the San Gabriel Mountains, with "diggings" established in both Placerita and Big Santa Anita Canyons.

Benjamin D. Wilson, Yankee entrepreneur and beloved gringo adopted by the principally Spanish- speaking Angeleno population as Don Benito, was the first to penetrate the mountains. The road he constructed climbed precipitously to the top of the mountain which today bears his name.

Built for the purpose of reaching the tall timber that flourished on the mountain tops, Don Benito's project was completed in 1864. During the brief decade to come, many others would follow— each endeavoring to exploit the region's many natural resources.

By the 1870's, summer droughts and winter floods began to plague the Los Angeles basin as a direct result of overcutting in the San Gabriel timberlands and the burning off of brush to create better rangelands for cattle. With the Colorado River aqueduct still decades away, the runoff from the snowfields of the San Gabriels provided the County with its single major source of water. Public outrage mounted as the devastation of mountain watershed began to affect the crops and business establishments in the valleys below.

SAN GABRIEL HIGH COUNTRY

In 1892, under the newly established Timberland Reserve Act, Congress set aside the San Gabriels as the first protected forest in America. The region's mere designation as a reserve, however, did not in any way afford the protection required to maintain and enhance its resources. The holocaust of one devastating fire after another left the range permanently denuded of precious woodlands and forests.

Today, the San Gabriels are vigorously protected by a complex and efficient organization of forestry personnel and firefighters. The Angeles Forest, as it has come to be known, encompasses more than 690,000 acres,

Majestic Mount San Antonio (*opposite page*), *referred to locally as Mount Baldy, rises to an elevation of over 10,000 feet above the sea. America's first government funded ranger station (below) still stands in a forested recess of the Angeles National Forest (above).*

Rangers are kept busy patrolling its 496 miles of riding and hiking trails, 99 campgrounds, 32 picnic areas, 844 summer residences, 42 organizational camps, and 7 winter sports areas. Watershed protection and recreation seem to be today's priorities for the Forest Service, with great efforts being made to restore timberlands and to protect and enhance the mountain's population of tenacious wildlife.

In addition to a large number of mule deer, it is estimated that the San Gabriel Mountains continue to support a population of some 300 bighorn sheep, 50 black bears, and perhaps 15 mountain lions. Smaller wildlife, too, is abundant, although skittish, due to the constant onslaught of poachers throughout the region.

Bighorn Sheep (opposite page and above) thrive in the isolated canyons and higher elevations of the San Gabriel wilderness, while a significant population of California Black Bear (usually cinnamon or brown in color) roam much of the areas forested regions.

RACCOON

New threats challenge the Forest Service, such as the fatal effect of air pollutants on stands of high country pines and the weekend onslaught of urbanites seeking refuge in a wilderness that they are threatening to destroy through their careless contributions of litter and forest fires.

MULE DEER

MEADOW AT CHILAO

MT. BALDY

As early as 1891, the Los Angeles Chamber of Commerce envisioned the pristine wilderness of the San Gabriels as "a great park" that would serve future generations of Angelenos. This vision has grown to have even greater significance at a time when Southern California wildlands have drastically diminished in size and quality. The present generation will face the challenge not only to maintain but to restore to its original splendor one of God's greatest gifts to Los Angeles—the San Gabriel Wilderness.

MORMON ROCKS

DESERT SIDE OF THE SAN GABRIELS

4. Suburban Los Angeles

DON TORMEY

CRAIG AURNESS

CRAIG AURNESS

At night from above, the freeways of Los Angeles appear like mighty rivers flowing over mountain passes and spilling their contents into a vast sea of cities. Many have traveled these routes in search of their own offramp to happiness.

From the Civic Center, LA's suburbs stretch out for nearly 60 miles in all directions. Francis Lloyd Wright lamented that the Southern California country- side had been raped by the rapid encroachment of urban development. Overwhelmed by the post-World War II "sun-rush," it is true that the Southland has sacrificed much in order to provide housing and opportunities for the millions who have chosen to settle here. At the same time, it is remarkable that of this seemingly endless migration of newcomers, a rapid assimilation to and concern over the adopted motherland has given birth to a new generation of Angelenos more concerned over the welfare of their communities and natural resources than perhaps even the native sons and daughters of the city.

CRAIG AURNESS

DON TORMEY

CRAIG AURNESS

In attempting to decipher LA, many a writer has found himself swept away in line after line of descriptive phrases concerning the oddities and unusual subcultures of the city. He finds himself at the end of his article without ever having mentioned the average and entirely straight scenes and individuals that make up the bulk of what LA really is all about. Above all else, and in spite of all the Hollywood hype, LA is one big "hometown USA," full of civic-minded citizens who are concerned about public schools, property taxes, and religious commitments. For these millions of typical American families, this giant megalopolis is not a mere sprawling expanse of urbanity but rather a series of small-town independent communities, each with boundaries and landmarks that set it apart from the rest.

The mass market environment herein created has made the American dream accessible to more families than ever before. With the nation's highest standard of living, predictions are that by 1989 LA's economy will have continued to grow faster than the rest of the nation's — adding 1.5 million new jobs and boosting the average family income to $30,000.

SUBURBAN LOS ANGELES **93**

A recent survey conducted by the Los Angeles Times indicated that Angelenos are more satisfied with their city and its services than people living in comparable metropolitan areas. They feel safer in their neighborhoods, have greater confidence in the honesty and reliability of civil servants, believe their minorities are treated better, and are convinced that their city offers the finest in recreational facilities and entertainment.

The good life is what the people of Los Angeles are trying to attain. Actor Jack Lemmon describes his awakening to the amenities of LA thusly: "I remember one of my first mornings here, as long as I live I'll never forget it. I had a little second-hand MG and a little apartment in Westwood, and driving into town on Sunset, I looked up and there were the mountains on a clear morning with snow on top and I was sitting in a T-shirt and the ocean was behind me." Journalist John Gregory Dunne expressed his idea of LA this way: "When I think of Los Angeles now, after almost a decade and a half of living not only in it but with it, I sometimes feel an astonishment,

an attachment, that approaches joy. I am attached to the way the palm trees float and recede down empty avenues, attached to the deceptive perspectives of the pale subtropical light. I am attached to the drydocks of San Pedro . . . and to the refineries of Torrance, which at night resemble an extraterrestrial space station . . . I am attached to the particular curve of coastline as one leaves the tunnel at the end of the Santa Monica Freeway to drive north on the Pacific Coast Highway. I am attached perhaps especially to the time warp of Boyle Heights and Echo Park and Silver Lake.''

Each week an average of 700 new residents settle in the greater Los Angeles basin. Like those before them, most have come seeking an opportunity for health, happiness and prosperity. All will shortly become acutely aware of the dues they must pay should they decide to stay. For paradise to be had, there is a price that must be paid. Civic responsibilities and political and social obligations must not be shunned. The mere burden of maintaining the quality of life for so many is an overwhelming task.

JAMES BLANK

CRAIG AURNESS

CRAIG AURNESS

The first to migrate to Los Angeles were the Spanish. As with all transplanted residents since, they attempted to re- create the environment of their homeland, planting palm trees and olive orchards and constructing communities typical of those found in Spain. Their two principal outposts, the missions San Gabriel and San Fernando, still stand today and provide Angelenos with a nostalgic and reverent reminder of the religious beginnings of their communities.

CRAIG AURNESS

CRAIG AURNESS

PHOTOS: CRAIG AURNESS

   Forest Lawn is a typical example of the way that Los Angeles exploits even the most sacred rites of civilization. Without a doubt one of the world's outstanding memorial parks, one nonetheless gets the feeling that he is in a Hollywood movie with the Savior playing the lead role. To avoid sounding disrespectful, it must be said for the record that when the author himself passes away he, too, hopes to find his final resting place atop the beautiful hills of Forest Lawn.

LA is and always has been a fun place to be—providing some of the world's most outstanding entertainment attractions. Although not officially the home of Disneyland (Anaheim being an LA suburb, but belonging under the jurisdiction of neighboring Orange County), Los Angeles can lay claim to Magic Mountain, a crackerjack amusement park boasting of the greatest rollercoasters and thrill attractions (referred to as "the great whiteknucklers") to be found anywhere. Live entertainment, nightly fireworks, and fine restaurants add to the enchantment of the park, delighting both locals and out-of-towners alike.

CRAIG AURNESS

In Los Angeles something special is always going on—be it the authentically re-created annual Renaissance Fair, held on the old Paramount movie ranch, or the yearly Easter Sunrise Service at the Hollywood Bowl. Topping the bill of extravaganzas is the world-reknowned Tournament of Roses Parade in Pasadena, followed by the heated com-

DON TORMEY

DON TORMEY

CRAIG AURNESS

petition of the Rose Bowl Game. First held on New Year's Day back in 1890, the now-famous pageantry of the tournament—with its magnificent floral floats, brass bands, and celebrites —today attracts a world-wide audience numbering in the millions.

CRAIG AURNESS

CRAIG AURNESS

The Magnificent Huntington Library and Estate *(above) houses a priceless collection of art, sculpture, and literary works, including the famous painting of Blue Boy (lower left corner). Other outstanding displays can be seen at the Norton Simon Museum in Pasadena (opposite page).*

Cultural opportunities are numerous and varied here, with outstanding collections of art and literary works being displayed at places such as San Marino's Huntington Library and Pasadena's Norton Simon Museum.

For the horticulturalist, the suburbs of LA offer an incredible montage of gardens, forests, and jungle—all created by man; the grandest being found in the LA County Arboretum. Originally planted on the estate of Lucky Baldwin, one of LA's first millionaires, this paradisical wonderland is now used not only for scientific research but as a lifelike set for many Hollywood productions— most recently having been used for the filming of the final sequence in the network blockbuster "Roots."

To live in LA is an experience unequal to living anywhere else in the world. Life takes on an unusual pace— daily routine is disrupted by a constantly changing environment. It is a challenge, to say the least, to try and keep up with a city like Los Angeles. Perhaps for this reason many have resorted to throwing in the towel and setting out to lead life their own way. Such a philosophy leads to the bizarre variety of lifestyles found here and often brings chaotic results. But, contrary to popular belief, most Angelenos manage to maintain a high standard of social conduct, unimpaired by the future shock effects of their city; and thanks to them, LA remains a great place to call "home."

5. City of the Angels

CRAIG AURNESS

JAMES BLANK   CRAIG AURNESS

Like every other major metropolitan community in America, Los Angeles faces monumental socio-economic and environmental challenges daily. Her "skid row" and delapidated barrios are graphic examples of the impersonal "faceless city" syndrome that breeds poverty and crime in today's world. On the other hand, unlike most other major American cities, LA boasts of an incredible pool of talent and creative genius. A powerful and dynamic community, Los Angeles is constantly progressing—a city on the move that finds itself in a perpetual state of change. Innovation is the name of the game in a community impatient with precedence and anxious to press forward. Angelenos operate on a grand scale, taking seemingly insurmountable obstacles in stride and executing magnificent engineering feats with flair and imagination. Far-flung community groups are brought

CRAIG AURNESS

CRAIG AURNESS

CRAIG AURNESS

together by efficient county planning commissions and regional agencies. Their combined accomplishments are the envy of many cities of comparable size who find themselves unable to muster civic pride and to overcome jealousies between the inner-city and their suburbs.

Urban renewal and downtown renovation are the current projects of an undaunted LA city council. At the same time Cal Trans, an agency established to help maintain the most complex freeway system in the world, is busy setting up a computer network which will help to increase the capacity and fluency of the city's transportation corridors. In the lab, technicians and scientists are attempting to find a cure-all for the ills of air pollution. Trend-setting city of the 21st century, LA offers tremendous insight into—and possible solutions to—the problems that will soon beset the communities of the world.

Old Los Angeles, *with her historic Bradbury Building (top photo), Pershing Square (bottom photo), and onetime principal business district (opposite page).*

JAMES BLANK

New Los Angeles (*opposite page*) *features sleek skyscrapers, such as The Arco Towers (right hand corner photo) and modernistic designs such as the reconstructed Times Mirror Square (below).*

Standing starkly out of place against the redeveloped Bunker Hill District skyline of steel and glass skyscrapers are the brick and adobe structures of El Pueblo de Los Angeles. Looking like a Hollywood set in the midst of an otherwise very contemporary cityscape, the almost entirely restored birthplace of LA offers insight and access to a past that has long since vanished. Wandering through the open air marketplace along cobblestoned Olvera Street or exploring the Avila Adobe (oldest standing home in Los Angeles) and the city's first fire station offers unforgettable experiences that will transport the viewer—even if only for a moment—into another time when Spanish was the principal language spoken on the West Coast and big cities were a faraway phenomena.

From such beginnings, the City of the Angels has grown to become a truly international community. Close examination of the city's subcultures reveals significant colonies of Japanese (Little Tokyo) and Chinese (Chinatown), as well as large concentrations of blacks and Chicanos (Mexican Americans). More recently, the city has experienced an influx of refugees from Indo China and the Mideast. Today, it would be difficult to find a nationality that is not represented here.

Chinatown *affords westerners the opportunity to experience authentic oriental cuisine and to sample a lifestyle that in recent years has attracted much attention. Most colorful of all events held here is the exciting Chinese New Year's celebration with its parades, dragons, and fireworks.*

Located near the Civic Center is Little Tokyo, the world's largest Japanese colony. Luxurious hotel accommodations, fine restaurants and modern financial institutions give the community a clean contemporary look. Special holidays and colorful festivals are well attended each year by Angelenos of all nationalities.

The brainchild of Sabatino Rodia, *an Italian immigrant to the city of Los Angeles, Watts Towers stand as a symbol of creative energy and a memorial to both the artist and his adopted homeland; for as Rodia put it, "I wanted to do something for the United States because there are nice people in this country."*

Many have come to LA seeking the opportunity to obtain a good education, hoping to complete their studies and return to serve the government and institutions of their own countries. With internationally acclaimed schools of higher learning such as the University of Southern California and the University of California at Los Angeles, to name but a few, LA offers more educational opportunities to its youth and the students of the world than practically any other major American city.

WATER AND POWER BUILDING

Culturally speaking, LA nearly equals New York, as the arts here are vigorously supported by a paying public. In addition to the commercial ventures of Hollywood, Los Angeles is proud of her many serious and outstanding public and private collections of art. Showcase theaters such as the Schubert and the Huntington Hartford bring to the city the best of Broadway, while the dazzling Los Angeles Music Center serves as home for the city's own philharmonic orchestra.

MUSIC CENTER

LA's *ultramodern convention center plays host to a variety of con-
ference groups and trade shows throughout the year. Photograph
courtesy of Autoexpo '79.*

Sports are also an integral part of the LA scene, with Dodger baseball action heading up the list in popularity, followed by basketball with the Lakers and ice hockey with the Kings at the Fabulous Forum in Inglewood. Surprisingly enough, horse racing actually draws the largest crowds of any spectator sport, while the popularity of soccer continues to spread like wildfire across the suburbs. The Coliseum, long-time home of the Los Angeles Rams, will undoubtedly serve as the focal point for the upcoming Olympic games to be hosted by the city in 1984.

LA's civic playground is the 4,000-acre Griffith Park, offering everything from a golf course and bridle trails to the world-famous Los Angeles Zoo. With its wide expanses of green lawn and cool, refreshing groves of trees, the park is a welcome retreat from the bustling city beyond and serves as a gathering place for many local cultural functions and sporting events. Crowning jewel of the refuge is the exciting Griffith Park Observatory. Within this historic Hollywood landmark, one can experience a voyage into space during any one of a number of daily planetarium programs. In the evening, a dazzling series of laser shows begins—catapulting the guest into the realms of science fiction and fantasy to the beat of rock and disco music.

Stretching across the Valley to Westwood is the Wilshire District, financial epicenter of the West Coast. Begun in 1927 by the man whose name it bears, the "Miracle Mile"—as the project was optimistically tagged —has since become an extraordinary showcase of innovative business ventures and financial institutions, pioneering programs and designs such as district trade shows and synchronized traffic lights.

PHOTOGRAPH BY CRAIG AURNESS

JAMES BLANK

CRAIG AURNESS

CRAIG AURNESS

CRAIG AURNESS

CRAIG AURNESS

Within or near the Wilshire district *are such notable attractions as (from top to bottom) the County Art Museum, La Brea Tar Pits and George C. Page Museum, Farmer's Market, and the University of California at Los Angeles. The district also serves as an architectural showcase for the West Coast, with its array of spectacular financial centers, office building complexes, and beautiful churches.*

Holy Temple
in the
City of the Angels

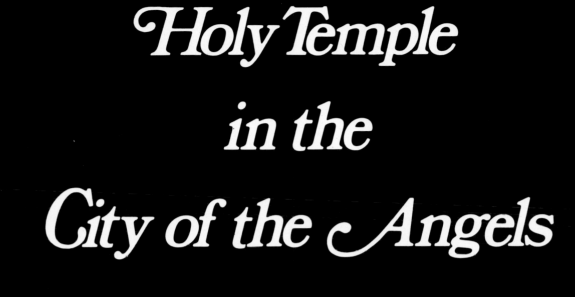

CREATION ROOM

BAPTISMAL FONT

Rising above the city, on a hill overlooking Santa Monica Boulevard, is the majestic Mormon Temple. Home of the largest such colony outside of the Rocky Mountains, LA has shared its history with that of the Church of Jesus Christ of Latter-day Saints since the Mexican-American War, when Mormon soldiers commissioned by the U.S. government transformed much of the ramshackled pueblo into an upstart of a Yankee community. Like the city's Jewish population, Mormons continue to stand out as one of LA's most dynamic religious entities. Their temple, focal point of every Latter-day Saint community, is actually larger than its world-renowned counterpart in Salt Lake City and serves not as an ordinary meeting house but rather as a sacred edifice wherein priesthood ordinances are performed. Due to the sacred nature of these ordinances, guests are not allowed inside. A beautiful and informative Visitors Center, constructed adjacent to the temple, relates the life of Christ and explains the purpose of temple work through outstanding graphic displays and motion pictures.

PHOTOGRAPHS COURTESY OF THE CHURCH OF JESUS CHRIST OF LATTER DAY SAINTS

MARRIAGE ALTER

LA's international airport places the giant megalopolis within easy reach of the free world, with flights arriving daily from all four corners of the globe.

From her obscure birth as a tiny colony of New Spain, Los Angeles has risen to accept her position as the second largest city in America. In the years ahead, experts predict that she will become a regional capital of the nations of the Pacific, functioning as the world's single most significant marketplace.

6. Hollywood

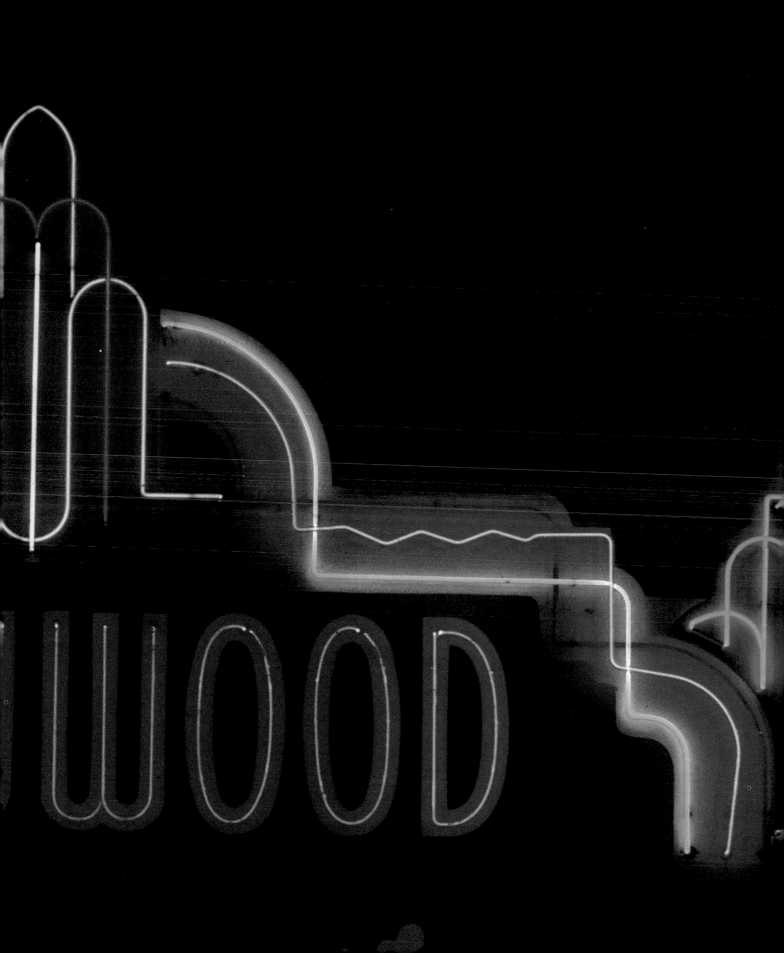

©METRO-GOLDWYN-MAYER

CRAIG AURNESS

JAMES BLANK

Hollywood's first motion picture was produced in a barn at the corner of Sunset and Gower back in 1910. From such humble beginnings, the legendary "Tinsel Town" evolved into today's "Entertainment Capital of the World," encompassing all facets of the business, from film making to the recording industry. A vibrant, pulsating town, Hollywood has outgrown her boundaries, as has the rest of Los Angeles, spilling over Cahuenga Pass into the San Fernando Valley and across Beverly Hills to Culver City. Within her walls lies the stuff of which dreams are made — idea factories — think tanks — wherein creative genius and the skills of storytelling combine to reach a climax in the ultimate art form. From the outside, Hollywood looks unpretentious enough. Tourists are frequently disappointed as they circle

CRAIG AURNESS

CRAIG AURNESS

© METRO-GOLDWYN-MAYER

the perimeters of barbwire-fenced studios and cruise down boulevards that look little different than those of their own hometowns. But hidden behind thick walls and tucked into the canyons of the Hollywood Hills are the dreamers, the hustlers, the brilliant artists, who have created one of the world's most lucrative industries out of nothing more than the resources of the human brain and the celluloid upon which the imaginative flights of that brain are captured.

The town that made sunglasses fashionable and black limousines a status symbol is best remembered by millions the world over for having made dreams come true. Indeed, Hollywood is a personal experience— for its product has touched our lives and played a significant role in making us

think, act, and dress the way that we do for over 70 years. Names such as Mary Pickford, Charles Chaplin, Mae West, and Clark Gable muster private memories and often bring a nostalgic tear to the eye — not necessarily for the genius of the film recollected but for the connection drawn between that movie and our own experience of that time as lovers, soldiers in combat, or ambitious youngsters striving to make our own dreams come true. The silver screen continues to enchant and enhance the quality of our lives as major studios and independent producers today turn out the biggest blockbusters of all time. For it seems that just as we have come as far as we can, Hollywood catapults our imaginations further into the realms of creativity with films like Star Wars and Superman.

CRAIG AURNESS

Studio budgets today have skyrocketed, just as has the attendance of moviegoers, with each studio striving to accomplish the ultimate in cinematography and special effects. Such vitality in the industry has produced the best and highest- grossing films ever to come forth from Hollywood's film labs since her pre- World War II golden era.

Re- makes such as Heaven Can Wait and The Champ prove the longevity of a good story, while innovative adaptations of earlier film classics such as The Wiz illustrate the ever- changing nature of the entertainment industry as it strives to keep itself one step ahead of the public's expectations.

THE WORLD FAMOUS HOLLYWOOD BOWL

PHOTOGRAPH BY CRAIG AURNESS

indeed, much of what Los Angeles is all about stems from the fact that she is the home of the industry and the birthplace of many of Hollywood's most spectacular fantasies. Several major studios, Universal being the most notable, offer both public and private tours; and by contacting an independent production company, one can often attend the actual filming of a motion picture and meet the stars themselves up close. Of course, running

RANDY COLLINGS

THE WIZ

into Barbra Streisand in a chance encounter or catching a camera crew in action on the street is still a very real possibility. For such occurrences, Hollywood is, indeed, an exciting place to be. Although one sees many a broken life represented on her Walk of Fame (a two-mile stretch of star-studded sidewalk), as success and failure do walk hand in hand down Hollywood Boulevard, yet the chance of someday making it big, of becoming an overnight success, penetrates the aura of this community with a hope well-substantiated by many who have persisted and achieved.

During Hollywood's greatest and most successful era, when more than 600 feature films were being ground out of her studios each year, this town came to face her greatest

Recent Hollywood block busters *have included such motion pictures as* **Superman** *and*

Star Wars, *while remakes of classic films such as* **The Champ** *prove the longevity of a good story.*

Hollywood's studio backlots (*above and below*) *stretch out across the San Fernando Valley. On the Universal Studios tour* (*lower left corner*) *guests are taken behind the scenes on the largest motion picture studio in the world.*

At Mann's Chinese Theater (*above and below*) *and along Hollywood's walk of fame (lower right corner) one can recapture the excitement of Hollywoods golden era with its movie greats and gala premieres.*

Century City's ABC entertainment center, *showcase for the media, with its many Hollywood premieres, Broadway musicals, and film festivals.*

© NBC

© NBC

© NBC

challenge. The birth of television wrecked havoc among the studios as millions opted to stay home and enjoy the inexpensive luxury of "the tube." Heated competition persisted for years between the networks and the majors. Thousands of theaters were forced to close their doors forever. Not until the

televised broadcast of the Academy Awards ceremony in 1953, and the record-breaking attendance of moviegoers which followed, did the two mass media giants realize the great possibilities of working together in a mutually beneficial relationship.

The television studio today is the most prominent entity in Hollywood. Indeed, The Johnny Carson Show has become one of this community's major tourist attractions. Complimentary tickets to the taping of most situation comedies and variety shows are easily attained from any of the major networks or local stations.

© NBC

© ABC

© CBS

Outdistancing both the networks and the studios is the recording industry, which annually grosses more in sales than either of the other entertainment entities, with over half of all dollars made coming into Hollywood from markets outside of the United States. Although born in New York, like the motion picture industry itself, disco and other contemporary sounds are marketed by Los Angeles to an international audience—with groups such as the Bee Gees, Donna Summer, and Village People setting trends for the future evolution of popular music.

Most recording studios are situated on or near Sunset Boulevard, a slick strip of nightclubs and penthouse suites whose most outstanding attractions are not necessarily the groups that entertain here but the fantastic billboards and neon signs that tower above the street, glamorizing the latest recording hits.

Posh Beverly Hills and Bel Air lie just beyond, with their meticulously manicured landscapes and spectacular homes. One could spend days driving up and down Stone Canyon Road or Beverly Glen Boulevard and still be continually fascinated by the ongoing array of picturesque cottages and stately mansions.

PHOTOGRAPH BY RANDY COLLINGS

Magnificent estates, *and beautiful homes adorn Hollywood's showcase residential communities of Beverly Hills and Bel Air.*

Along Rodeo Drive, in the heart of the Beverly Hills shopping district, one will encounter the West Coast's home of high fashion and the birthplace of that internationally sought-after "California look." Shops and boutiques here cater to the casual yet elegant lifestyle of Southern California's upper

echelon. Nestled beneath super-structures of glass and steel, the crisp, well-tailored facade of each individual shop, often adorned with uniformed doormen and parking attendants, creates an environment that even the courtiers of Rome, London, and Paris would be hard pressed to match.

No chapter on Hollywood would be complete without making some mention of Walt Disney's Magic Kingdom. Originally designed to be built adjacent to the Disney Studios in Burbank, Walt's "theme-park" entertainment concept soon outgrew its own drawing board and wound up in rural Anaheim where enough land was available for a studio backlot the size of Universal Pictures. It was Disney's desire to create a showplace for Hollywood—something for tourists to see when they came to town.

To call Walt's dream an amusement park is an absurdity, for Disneyland today no more resembles Coney Island than does the Huntington Library. Disneyland is Hollywood—a series of walk-on movie sets wherein the guest can actively participate in one themed adventure after another, as if playing the lead role in a motion picture. In fact this was precisely how the staff at Disney Studios designed the park back in the early 1950's. Each attraction was laid out on a "storyboard," as is done with a motion picture production, and a sequence of events was established to carry the guest from one scene to the next.

Pioneering new fields in entertainment is what Hollywood is all about. With such innovations as video disc recording and Disney's "audio-animatronics" being developed, it is certain that the Entertainment Capitol of the World will continue to dazzle future generations with as much creativity and genius as she has done for us in her glorious past.

EPILOG:

LOS ANGELES IN THE 25TH CENTURY

Many feel that the conclusion to this book should read as an epitaph rather than an epilog—those who profess the doom of the late great city of LA, basing their beliefs on geologic fact. The unique and varied topography of Southern California is due in part to her many active earthquake faults, which over the years have thrust up mountains and created a rugged coastline. While some such movements have occurred on a violent catastrophic scale, most have come about over the eons or time through subtle, small-scale tremors and shifting. Guestimations by those who have made serious study of the creation of her landscape indicate that Los Angeles is presently due for another "big shake." Such a prophecy does not justify the popularly held notion that the entire City of the Angels will some day slip into the sea as a result of a violent earthquake the likes of which has never been recorded in modern history.

A realistic appraisal of the situation reveals that the city of Los Angeles, as she continues to grow and progress, must be ever cognizant of the inevitable, constructing homes and business facilities that will be able to withstand the stress of tremors. Houses precariously situated on steep hillsides and improperly constructed high-rise facilities invite tragedy and should therefore be outlawed by the County Planning Commission. Criminal actions should be taken against those who court disaster by locating major housing developments directly on top of known faultlines.

A long-range view of the future of today's super-city is exciting enough to astonish even the most avid science fiction fanatic. As if from a scene in Buck Rogers, the cityscape that will undoubtedly evolve reveals a network of developments that conserve energy, create acres of open space, and flow with the movement of the earth.

In his book "City of the Angels," author Richard Gilbert takes a look at some of the fascinating and provocative concepts that are already shaping LA's future. Quoting studies made at UCLA, Gilbert predicts "the end of the traditional American axis running from East to West which has left the Eastern states in a position of political, cultural, and economic control over the country. On this axis, the West Coast is just the end of a long line." Today, a new axis is emerging as a result of the growth of the American Northwest, LA's close proximity to trade-hungry China—as well as to the export/import-minded Japanese—and her ties with the recently politically significant Mexico and the whole of Latin America. Contracts already exist with Los Angeles firms to explore the undeveloped eastern frontiers of the Soviet Union for petroleum and other natural resources. LA's great aerospace industry today dominates the future of air and space travel. From all of these developments—and many more—one might easily conclude that the future will witness the growth of a Pacific Basin culture and that the center of this "new axis" will be found in Southern California.

Los Angeles has already begun to assume her role as the capital of a new regional hierarchy of economic and political power. The most important metropolis of the western United States by a huge margin and the great production center and marketplace of the Pacific Rim, LA and her remarkably diversified industries will inevitably remain as a world showcase for progress and development during the millenium to come.

Evolution of a City

Straight line "cities" for 200 mph rapid transit. One "city" may be multiple miles long—with greenbelts surrounding.

Skyscrapers'—inefficient traffic patterns

Capsules: Individual transits computerized into chain to travel 200 mph.

Individual & group people mover.

Capsules compute in and out.

Then compute off onto tributaries to travel independantly at 30 mph.

Use of earth's constant temperature for energy efficiency

Already boasting of the nation's largest underground shopping complex, much of the city's development in the years ahead will most likely take place beneath the surface of the earth, with above-ground structures blanketed in lush vegetation and rich topsoils, creating a scene more reminiscent of rambling hills than urban sprawl. Such design will not only conserve energy, made necessary for heating and cooling, but will also enhance the environment, reclaiming vast tracts of open space from urban blight. A spectacular vista will emerge, unobliterated by unsightly structures; woodlands, lakes, wild game reserves, and parks will stretch from the sea inland across the basin to the San Gabriel Mountains and the desert beyond.

Los Angeles has always been a city of dreamers and doers. Beneath the tinsel of Hollywood, one encounters many of the most creative geniuses of our time. Each new day in LA sees the birth, development, and marketing of new and original concepts, offered to an idea-starved world. One can only hope that such potential talent and innovation will find direction and not be squandered in this gentle environment that all too often encourages "laid back" complacency rather than aggressive crusades. Possessing all of the tools necessary to solve many of the ills of today's world—as well as tomorrow's—LA remains as America's window into the future. Like a Hollywood production, she has created for us a vision in miniature of the marvelous possibilities that the future holds. To grasp the dream and pursue it is the challenge awaiting every child of the City of Angels.

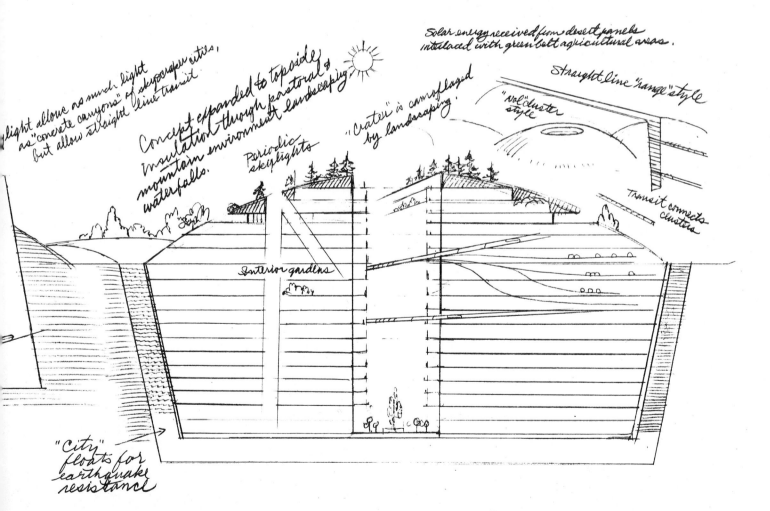

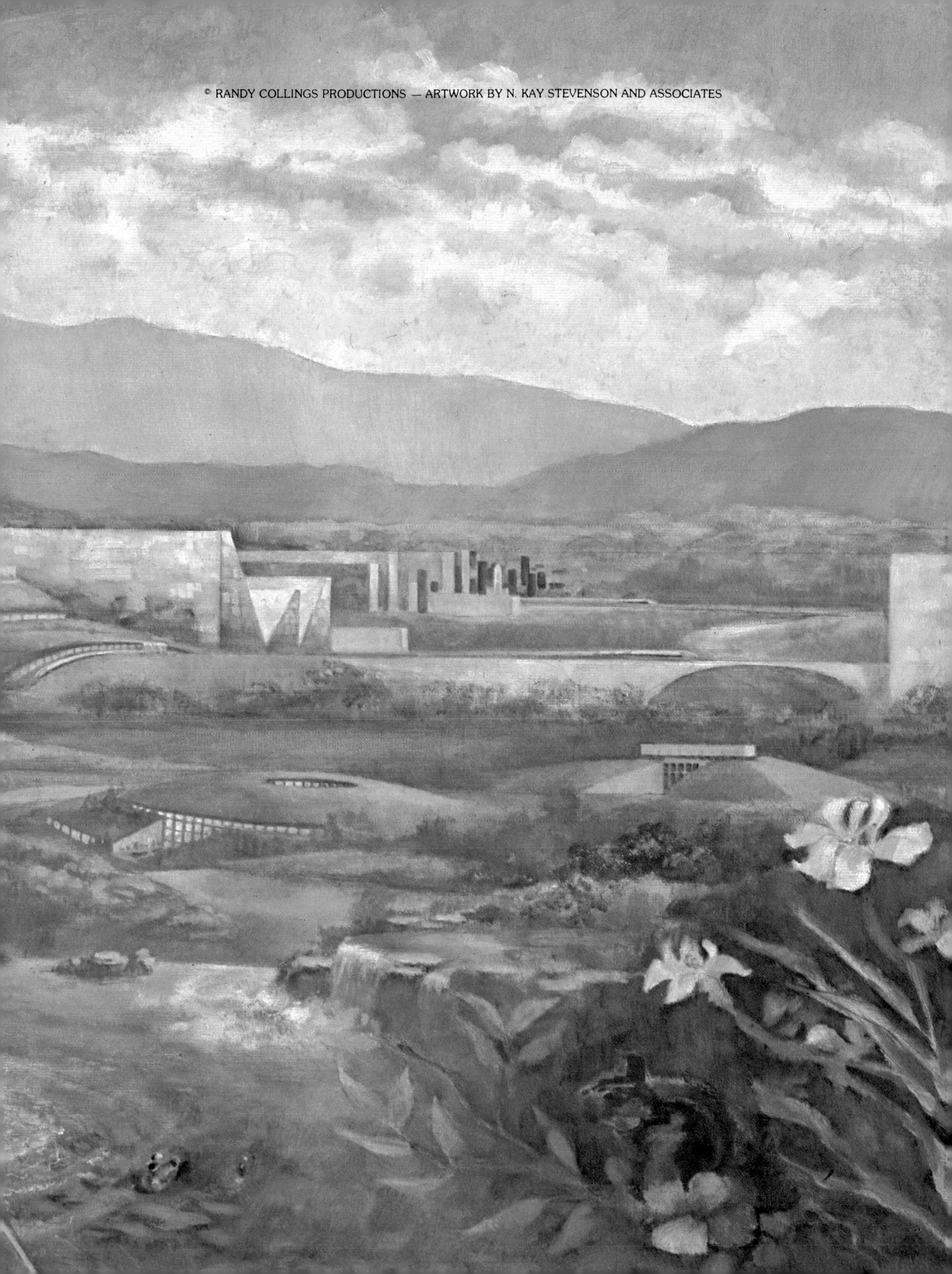

INDEX

Figures in italic denote illustrations.

This book was printed by Continental Graphics, Los Angeles, California from Litho Film pre-
pared by Angel Photo Color Service, Inc., North Hollywood, California. Body type and type
for heads was composed by Publishers Typesetting, Anaheim, California. Paper for pages
is Sonoma Gloss made by Zellerbach.

THE END
Randy Collings Productions